Tropical Trees
of
Hawaii

布哇熱帶樹

Text and Color Photography

by

Dorothy and Bob Hargreaves

First Printing 1964
Copyright in Japan / Dorothy and Bob Hargreaves

Published by
ROSS-HARGREAVES
A Division of L. & M. Equipment Co. Inc.
P.O. Box 11897 LAHAINA, HAWAII 96761 U.S.A.

AFRICAN TULIP TREE, Flame of the Forest, Fountain Tree アフリカン チユリツフ

Spathodea campanulata BEAUVOIS

A large, colorful tree (see cover) discovered by Palisot Beauvois on the Gold Coast of Africa in 1787. Its fiery red flowers grow in circular groups around closely crowded buds as seen in the picture above. These buds develop a few at a time thus insuring blooms the year around. It is called the Fountain Tree because the unopened buds will spurt compressed water when pinched between the fingers. Birds are often startled upon receiving a spray of water if their beak pierces a bud. Youngsters use them as water pistols. You will see the tree all over the islands. There is an avenue of trees on University Avenue at Kaala St.

AUTOGRAPH TREE, Copey, Scotch Attorney クルシア

Clusia rosea Jacq.

A West Indian tree with magnificent large thick ovate leaves 3″ x 8″. The tree resists salt spray and high winds. Its 2″ to 4″ white flowers, delicately shaded with pink have a hard center and open from tightly closed deep pink buds. An interesting non-edible 3″ fruit can be dried for arrangements. Medicine is obtained from the leaves, bark, and fruit. In the West Indies, the leaves were marked and used for playing cards. Perhaps a Scotch attorney used these. Today, lovers and children delight in leaving their autographs on a young leaf and then watching the leaf grow. (See inset.) Kailua Post Office Plaza, University of Hawaii, Police station entrance on Young Street, many yards.

AVOCADO
Alligator Pear   アボカド

Persea americana MILL
The first trees in Hawaii were said to have been planted by Don Marin. Deciduous trees that bear when 4 to 8 years old for about 25 years, 500 or more fruits a year. Guatemalan type—warty, hard, nut like flavor, yellow like butter, contains up to 30% oil, rich in vitamins, used for lighting, soap, medicine, cosmetics, and food. West Indian type—green or purplish leathery, smooth, thin skin. University of Hawaii, State Hospital, private yards.

4

BANANA TREE, Mai‘a

バナナノキ

Musa (over 70 species, over 300 edible forms)

An old Hawaiian proverb likens man to the banana: "Man is like a banana the day it bears fruit"—like the banana which dies after it bears its one bunch of bananas, man dies after his work is done.

After the Banana Tree bears, the new shoots (called keikis—babies in Hawaii) around the base of the tree soon grow into another tree to replace the one that dies. Banana Trees are used for food, roofs, cattle feed, clothing, medicine, dye, alcohol, wine, vinegar, and packing material. Many groves can be seen—Wilson Tunnel Highway on Windward Side of Oahu cuts through a large grove. Hawaii does not export bananas.

BANYAN—800 species *ficus* (Fig)

ヒス カス

INDIAN BANYAN, Vada Tree (above)—(*Ficus benghalensis* L.) from Hindu traders named Banyans. It is an evergreen from India sacred to the Hindus. The aerial roots (below) grow earthward from horizontal branches supporting the tree so that it covers large areas. In India one measured 2000′—85′ high. Iolani Palace, Moana Courtyard, Thomas Square, Kapiolani Park.

Banyan (cont.)

BO TREE, Peepul Tree, Sacred Tree

インド ボダイジユ

Ficus religiosa L.

This smooth grey trunked tree was brought from India in 288 BC to Ceylon. It is the oldest historical tree known—the parent of all still flourishing in Ceylon. Planted beside each Buddhist temple because Buddha meditated under a Bo tree for 6 years. The heart shaped 3″ to 7″ leaves above are a close up of the tree in Foster Gardens propagated from the tree under which Buddha sat. The full tree pictured was planted by the first graduating class at the University of Hawaii on the campus in 1911-12.

FIDDLE-LEAF FIG, Lyrata Fig   ヒスカス

Ficus lyrata Warb.

This handsome tree with lush, large, large, dark green leaves is often seen in yards in Hawaii. It is a native of Trop. Africa growing to about 35′ and it derives its common name from the fiddle shaped foot long leaves. The fruit is about 2″ (see close up). Kailua Post Office Parking Area, and Plaza.

Handsome grey barked tree from Trop. Indo-Pacific with ovate 6″ to 18″ leaves at branch ends where the fragrant flowers also cluster. The 5″ to 7″ brushlike blooms, white stamens with pink tips,

BARRINGTONIA, Hutu (Fish Poison Tree) ゴバンノアシ

Barringtonia asiatica (L.) Kurz.
syn. *B. speciosa* Forst.

open in the evening and fall in the morning. The heart shaped brownish quadrangular 4″ fruits contain seeds which are grated and cast into the water to stun fish. Husk is waterproof, buoyant, used for fishnet floats. Tahitians call it Hutu (or Hotu) meaning heart because of its shape. (Leaves similar to a Kamani—see page 31) Foster Gardens, University of Hawaii.

9

BEACH HELIOTROPE, Tahinu モンパノキ

Messerschmidia argentea (L.f.)
Johnston, syn. *Tournefortia
argentea* L.f.

An umbrella shaped tree up to 20′
with leaves clustered at the ends of
its branches. They are large ovate
and thick covered with silky white
hairs. The small white flowers (seen
in bud at the top of the picture at
right) are followed by the fruits
that look like tiny coiled goose-
berries on the spike hanging below. In India the leaves are eaten
raw as they have a parsley like
flavor. The tree withstands salt
spray so is found in great num-
bers near the ocean.

BREADFRUIT, 'Ulu

Artocarpus incisus (Thumb) L. f.
パンノキ

The breadfruit tree was brought in by the early Polynesians from Tahiti. From Malaysia, plants were taken by Captain Bligh on the Bounty in 1788. A 30' to 60' lovely tropical tree with exotic split leaves ranging from 1' to 3' long. Fruits usually ripen in June to August. They are about 5" to 8", weighing up to 10 lbs. The wood was used for canoes; bark for tapa; sap to fill in the seams of canoes and to catch birds. One or two breadfruit trees provided food enough for a year. The fruit is high in carbohydrates, is a source of Vitamin A, B, and C. University of Hawaii, Hawaii State Hospital.

11

BUTTERCUP TREE, Wild Cotton, Yellow-silk Tree

コツクロストマム

Cochlospermum vitifolium (Willd.) Spreng.

From Tropical America this tree is outstanding because of its bright yellow blossoms that resemble large buttercups. After the five 3″ to 5″ poppy-like petals fade, the fruit capsule of about 3″ forms. This contains a number of kidney shaped seeds

covered with long white floss—the "cotton or silk" of the tree. This is often used like kapok for stuffing pillows and mattresses. The tree is deciduous, usually blooming when leafless. The grapevine-like leaves give it the Latin name viti (grape) folium (leaf). Foster Gardens, Dowsett Avenue.

CALABASH TREE, La'amia フフベノキ

Crescentia cujete L.

An unusual tropical American tree with a short trunk and long spreading branches. The leaves seem to jut out from these branches. It has rather unpleasant smelling 2″ x 3″ flowers that are yellow with purple. The roundish fruits from 5″ x 12″ in diameter (note on tree below) first turn yellow, then brown. The hard shells can be beautifully polished—see picture at right. These gourds are used as Maracas in Mexico, South America and Spain, but in Hawaii they are used for feather gourds. (The seeds of the Canna Lillies—Li'ipoe, are placed in the shells for these hula rattles.) The gourds can be trained into different shapes by tying them when green. Foster Gardens, Likiliki Street by Archive Bldg., Lusitana Street.

CHICLE TREE, Chico, Sapodilla, Chewing Gum Tree

サボジラ

Achras zapota L. syn. *Sapota achras* Mill.
now known as *Manilkara zapodilla* (Jacq.) Gilly.

An evergreen 15′ to 60′ high from Central America. It has smooth dark green oblong leaves 2″ to 5″ with small white flowers and round edible brown fruits about the size of a golf ball. (See above.) They contain small black shiny seeds. This is a favorite fruit in Tropical America, but the tree is noted particularly as it is a source of chicle for chewing gum. The gum is obtained by tapping the trees every 2 or 3 years. Each tree yields about 60 quarts of latex which is made into gum. Foster Gardens.

14

CHINABERRY TREE
ride of India, Indian Lilac, Bead Tree

センダン

Melia azedarach L.

The first seeds of this tree of the old world were said to have been brought to Hawaii in 1850 by Dr. J. P. Judd. The tree is more common on some of the neighbor islands than on Oahu. It seems to adapt itself to lava flows and wild places, but makes an excellent shade tree also. Fast growing to 40′, it blooms in the spring with giant clusters of pale pink or blue-lilac blossoms. Each has a tiny dark purple staminal tube. These flowers are very fragrant, smelling like lilac. The deciduous leaves are a glossy green with tapering tips. The tree produces abundant fruits about the

size of a cherry with a single stone. These are sometimes used as beads, giving the tree the name Bead Tree.

The wood is long lasting so is used for musical instruments. Other parts of the tree have medicinal purposes.

Legend has it that the Chinaberry Tree has been worshipped in the Temples of Persia, Malaya, and Ceylon for as long as man can remember, yet in some places in the world, it is considered a weed. Seen at University of Hawaii, near Armory, Nuuanu, Islands of Hawaii, Molokai.

CHRISTMAS-BERRY TREE, Wilelaiki シナス

Schinus terebinthifolius Raddi

Bright red berry-like fruits form in dense clusters on this tree in the fall, and last until January. The tree is a cousin to the pepper tree, but is a much sturdier tree with definite branches and coarser leaves. It grows like a weed in Hawaii as the seeds are scattered widely by the birds. It is useful for decorations because of the bright red fruits, especially during the Christmas season. Seen along Kailua Road, growing wild along many highways and in the hills behind Honolulu.

COFFEE TREE コーヒーノキ
Arabian Coffee, Kona Coffee

Coffea arabica L.

Another small tree, native of East Africa, brought to Hawaii by Don Marin in 1813. Effort to grow coffee in 1825 in Manoa Valley (where the University of Hawaii now stands) failed. Finally Rev. Samuel Ruggles brought it to Kona in 1828, but there was not an extensive crop until about 1850. Today Kona is the only area producing much coffee. Leaves are shiny, 3″ to 6″; flowers are very fragrant (related to the Gardenia); and the berries ripen in the fall when Kona children vacation to help harvest the crops. The pulp is then removed, bean dried, shelled, graded and stored to season, then roasted and ground. Delicious! Besides the many Coffee trees to be seen on Hawaii, some can be seen behind the House of Coral on Windward Oahu, Foster Gardens, across from Thomas Square.

COLVILLEA コルビリア

Colvillea racemosa Bojer
This tree from Africa was started by seeds which were brought into Hawaii in 1918. The rich orange blossoms burst into bloom in the fall when there aren't too many other trees blooming. It looks a little like a Poinciana (a relative), but the fern-like leaves are larger and the flowers grow in large clusters at the branch tips. The buds resemble huge orange clusters of grapes. These buds gradually pop open revealing the true flower with tiny stamens poking up. University of Hawaii, 2400 block of Pali Highway, Mauka side of Kalanianaole Highway near Kuliouou.

18

CORAL SHOWER TREE, Pink Shower シャハノキ

Cassia grandis L.f.

There are a number of lovely Shower Trees in Hawaii (see "Hawaii Blossoms"—
Hargreaves), however, the Coral Shower is the first Cassia to bloom·in the spring.
It has been cultivated in Hawaii since 1870, so at the end of March until May
many trees can be seen sprinkled throughout the islands.

It has striking coral-pink blossoms that are massed in clusters along the branches.
They soon fall, making a colorful carpet on the ground below.

The large black pods of 3′ contain seeds used for leis. Seen on highway leading
into Kaneohe, Liholiho St. between Wilder and Lunalilo, Manoa Valley, Nuuanu
Valley.

CREPE MYRTLE
Queen of Flowers

Lagerstroemia speciosa (L.) Pers.

オオバナサルスベリ

Speciosa comes from the Latin speciosus meaning pleasing to the eye. This beautiful deciduous tree, native of India where it is called Jarool, is pleasing to the eye. It is valued for its tough red timber, medicinal use, and ornamental beauty. Foster Gardens, Lisbon St. (Border.) University of Hawaii.

EARPOD, Elephant's Ear

エントロピア

Enterolobium cyclocarpum (Jacq.) Griseb.

A deciduous wide-canopied tree from Venezuela with a huge grey trunk and branches. Grows up to 125′ high with a trunk to 10′ in diameter. The timber ranges from wood like white pine to that like black walnut. Of the Mimosa family, it has feathery foliage. Blooms April or May. Pods are shiny dark brown shaped like a large ear 3″ to 4″—see picture. These contain seeds used for leis. They serve as food for cattle, and the young pods for human food. Wood used for canoes and cabinets, fruit and bark used for tannin, soap and medicine. Foster Gardens, University of Hawaii, Park at University Avenue at Kaala Street.

EUCALYPTUS, Gum Tree, Palepiwa (Ward off fever), Nuholani (New Holland or Australia); about 300 species of Eucalyptus.

ロブスタユーカリ

Native of Australia and Malaysia. Grown for reforestation, ornament, timber, gum, tannin·oil for medicine. About 50 species introduced into Hawaii for reforestation. One is the Swamp Mahogany *Eucalyptus robusta*, Sm. Thick alternate pointed leaves. Fruiting capsule (see picture), when dried, used for arrangements. Many seen on Pali Highway, blown by the trades. Grow to 300 feet.

FALSE WILI-WILI
Red Sandalwood Tree,
Bead Tree　ナンバンアカアズキ

Adenanthera pavonina L.

      A tall erect tree from Ceylon, Asia, with branches of fine feathery foliage high on the smooth grey trunk. The wood is strong and durable—called red sandalwood because it is sometimes substituted for real sandalwood. Although it is called False Wili-Wili, it is an entirely different species than the Wili-Wili (see Tiger's Claw, page 63). The tree has small yellow flowers, but the curling pods that can be seen scattered here and there on the tree above, are valued not only for dried flower arrangements, but for the useful round bright red seeds they contain (Barricari or Circassian seeds). Thomas Square, Park at King and Keeaumoku Sts. They are eaten and used as weights in Asia, but are used for jewelry in Hawaii—see picture (note Lauhala mat under lei).

GOLD TREE, Primavera, Sunshine Tree   キンノキ

Cybistax donnell-smithii Rose
(formerly a *Tabebuia*)

Throughout the tropical world, the gold tree is known as one of the strongest and largest of tropical trees. It is called Primavera (white mahogany) because of its highly valuable wood. A single cubic foot may weigh from 60 to 80 lbs. Few trees can surpass it for durability and few trees can surpass it for beauty when in bloom. It is said that after the tree has flowered, the rains can be expected. Member of Bignonia family from Tropical America. Moanalua Park, Foster Gardens, Dole St. At the base of the Gold Tree in picture is the Plumeria or Frangipani—popular lei flower.

GUAVA, Kuawa

バンジロウ   *Psidium guajava* L.

This small evergreen spreading tree, 25′, is a native of Tropical America. Common along roadsides and in waste places in Hawaii. They have prominently veined 3″ to 6″ oblong leaves, fragrant white 1″ flowers followed by lemon-like thin-skinned aromatic fruit. Introduced into Hawaii by Don Marin, now made into delicious jams, jellies, and juices containing iron, calcium, and Vitamin C.

25

HAU TREE
(Pronounced How)　オオハマボウ

Hibiscus tiliaceus L.

A book of trees wouldn't be complete without this gnarled tree of the "old world." It is a true hibiscus. Seen in jungle-like growth on the old Pali road, yet also seen neatly trained into arbors at clubs, parks and hotels. The hibiscus flowers are bright yellow in the morning, but turn dark red by evening when they fall. Used for outriggers, medicine, ropes.

HAWAIIAN TREE FERN シダノキ
Hapuʻu

Cibotium chamissoi Kaulf.

The common hapuʻu that the Hawaiian orchids and anthuriums are planted in comes from the Tree Fern. It grows abundantly in the forests of Hawaii, especially on the island of Hawaii. (Hawaii National Park.) The trees form a lacy roof overhead. The cool green fronds uncurl from the hapuʻu base which is covered with a soft golden brown silky material the Hawaiians call "pulu." This pulu has been used for stuffing pillows and mattresses.

Tiki gods are made from the hapuʻu (see left), also slabs are cut from it and used for fences, pathways, and orchid logs. The path seen above with the many bright Periwinkle (*Vinca*) flowers is in a forest park on Maui.

IRONWOOD, Australian Pine, She Oak, Toa, Beefwood モクマオウ

Casuarina equisetifolia L.

A leafless tree named for a large Australian bird called a Cassowary. The long, thin, drooping, dull green needles are tufted like the feathers of the bird. Some trees growing in Malaya are said to be several hundred years old. The Ironwood was introduced into Hawaii, however, less than 100 years ago. A. S. Cleghorn, father of Princess Kaiulani, planted the avenue of Ironwoods by Kapiolani Park in 1890.

The coastline seen behind the tree left is below Kalawao Park where the Hansen's Disease patients were first dumped ashore on Molokai. The tiny red tufted flowers appear in May and June, cones also (see picture below). Cones made into earrings resembling pineapples. Trees useful as wind breaks. Symbol of faithfulness.

JACARANDA, Fern Tree　　　　　　　　チカランダ

Jacaranda acutifolia Humb. and Bonpl.
syn. *J. mimosaefolia* Don., *J. ovalifolia* R. Br.

The cool blue blossoms of this large Bignonia from Brazil are a welcome sight in Hawaii from January through June. It is a lovely large tree with grey bark and handsome feathery leaves that resemble ferns forming a ceiling overhead. At the height of the blooming season in May and June, the little violet-blue bell-like blossoms fall, making a carpet of color under the tree. Manoa Valley, Nuuanu, Schofield Barracks. Pods used for jewelry.

JACK FRUIT TREE, Jac Fruit パラミツ

Artocarpus heterophyllus Lam. syn. A. integer (*Thunb.*) Merr.

A strange relative of the breadfruit tree comes from India and Malaysia, but is quite rare in Hawaii. It grows to a height of about 50'. The 6″ oblong leaves are not as attractive as the exotic leaves of the breadfruit tree, but the fruits are most unusual. They are one of the largest fruits known. They weigh up to 70 lbs., are about 1' to 3' long, borne all along the trunk of the tree.

These fruits are an important food in the Eastern Tropics. Although the ripe fruit has an unpleasant odor, the taste outweighs this drawback. The yellowish, soft, flaky, sweet pulp is eaten raw, boiled, or fried and is delicious in curries. The large white seeds are also delicious roasted, tasting something like chestnuts.

The wood, which is lemon-yellow at first but turns to a dark red mahogany as it ages, is excellent for cabinet work. Found on lower slopes of Tantalus, Foster Gardens. (Tree in picture by the Administrator's Office at the Kaluapapa Settlement, Molokai.)

KAMANI TREE, True Kamani, Alexandrian Laurel

テリハボク

Calophyllum inophyllum L.

This tall handsome 60′ tree, native of India, is part of Hawaiian history. It was sacred to the Polynesians, and is mentioned in old Hawaiian chants.

Produces the Punnai Nut (right above) collected in Ceylon as they yield Dilo Oil, used medicinally. Seen in many yards, Kailua and Kaneohe roadsides, University of Hawaii, Park at King and Keeaumoku Sts.

FALSE KAMANI
Tropical Almond,
Kamani Haole

Terminalia catappa L.

モモタマナ

Brought to the islands many years ago, this tree is beloved because of its large leaves (similar to the Hutu—page 9) that turn red before they fall, suggestive of Autumn leaves. Salt resistant, wide spreading, edible fruits (almond shaped). Thomas Square, Foster Gardens, Parks.

31

KAPOK
インドワタノキ
Silk Cotton Tree

Ceiba pentandra (L.) Gaertn.

One of the oldest Kapok trees in Hawaii is in Foster Gardens. Ceibas are huge, thick, grey trunked trees with branches sticking out at right angles. They are majestic shade trees. Often planted in the market square. Their leaves have 5 to 9 fingers; the creamy white 1″ flowers appear just before the leaves. Two months after they fall, black oblong seeds 3″ to 6″ form. These capsules contain the floss called kapok used to stuff mattresses, pillows, life preservers and upholstery. Tree in Park at King and Keeaumoku also.

KIAWE, Algaroba, Mesquite キアベ
(pronounce the W as a V in Kiawe)

Prosopis pallida formerly *P. chilensis* (Mol.) Stuntz also *P. juliflora* (SW.) DC.

This picturesque 60′ tree with lovely fern-like leaves, thorny branches, and interesting gnarled trunk has become one of the most valuable trees in Hawaii. Its original parent was raised from a seed brought to Hawaii by Father Bachelot in 1828 from the Royal Gardens in Paris.

It is used to reforest waste lands, produce fuel, lumber, charcoal, food, medicine, tannin, and its pale yellow flowers (see picture at right) that bloom in the spring, produce 200 tons of honey yearly. The wax bean-like yellow pods, containing 25% grape sugar, produce 500,000 bags of fodder annually.

Many Kiawe trees are seen in the arid areas, but some large Kiawes can be seen at Kapiolani Park, Bishop Museum, University of Hawaii.

33

KOA コア

Acacia koa Gray

This native of Hawaii is truly a monarch of forest trees. Growing to heights of 100′, it is one of the twelve best reforesting trees. Koa, called Hawaiian Mahogany, is now used extensively in Hawaii for furniture, wood-work, ukuleles, and novelties because of its beautiful red grained wood and was formerly used for canoes, surf boards, cala-bashes. It is said that when an early Hawaiian wished to choose a Koa tree for a canoe, he found one which the 'elepaio bird had not been pecking. Seen in Hawaiian forests, Nuuanu and Manoa Valleys.

KOU, Cordia, Kou Haole, Geiger Tree チシャノキ

Cordia sebestena L.

As this evergreen tree from Tropical America flowers almost continuously, it is used widely for ornamental purposes. The wood of an indigenous Kou of Polynesia, *Cordia subcordata* Lam. was used by the early Hawaiians to make cups, dishes and calabashes.

The Kou thrives near the sea, and requires little water. The tubular flowers of about 1″ are frilled and crepe-like, and produce 1″ round white edible fruits. The rough oval leaves 3″ to 8″ long furnish shade the year around. Parts of tree used medicinally. Found in many beach home areas. University of Hawaii, Kailua Post Office Plaza.

KUKUI, Candlenut Tree

ククイノキ

Aleurites moluccana (L.) Willd.

Brought to the islands by early Polynesians who used the Kukui Nut oil for stone lamps, kernels strung on coconut midribs for candles, and husks and roots for tapa cloth dye. Can easily be noted in valleys and woods by its silvery green foliage which has 8″ maple-shaped leaves, small clusters of flowers (flower of Molokai), and 2″ green fruits (below left). These nuts are made into leis (below right—note royalty fishhook); kernels used for varnish, medicine, relish ('inamona), and fertilizer. Kukui on Iolani Palace grounds planted by President Roosevelt in 1934. The Kukui is the official tree emblem for the State of Hawaii.

This ancient tree from Polynesia, Australia, and Malaya is found everywhere in Hawaii.

The odd aerial roots give the tree the appearance of walking—called Walking trees. This is said to be a symbol of the many root stocks in Hawaii.

Tour drivers point out the "pineapples" in the Pandanus Tree. The drupes of these fruits are made into leis. They formerly were used as brushes to paint tapa cloth.

The name "Lauhala" refers to the leaves of this tree.

LAUHALA, Hala, Puhala, Pandanus, Screw Pine ラハラ

Pandanus odoratissimus L.f.

The 3′ leaves with their saw tooth edges are the most useful product of the tree. They are sturdy and pliable. The natives remove the curled end, prickly margin, and midrib, then dry the leaves, bleach them in salt water, and scrape them to soften the fiber (this can be seen done at Ulu Mau Village on Oahu). Mats for the floor, table, and walls are made of Lauhala (see mat on page 23). Natives also make baskets, purses, hats, sandals, and fans.

LIPSTICK TREE, Arnotto Dye Plant, Alaea　ベニノキ

Bixa orellana L.

Small Tropical American tree growing up to 30′ that has alternate heart-shaped 3″ to 7″ leaves, pink or white 2″ single flowers that resemble a wild rose, and two-valved 1″ to 2″ fruits. These are red, then turn brown and are covered with soft spines. They contain the 50 or so ovate scarlet seeds which yield bright yellow, tasteless dye called

Arnotto Dye once used to color margarine. It has vitamin value and has been used to color candy, chocolate, cloth, lips, oleo, paint, and soap. The bark furnishes a fiber for cordage, the stems eraser gum, and in Brazil bulls are fed the seeds and pulp to make them more dangerous in the bull ring. Now the seed pods are used extensively for dried floral arrangements. Old Pali Highway, University Avenue and Metcalf.

LITCHI NUT TREE　ライチ

Litchi chinensis Sonn.

The Litchi Tree was introduced to Hawaii in 1873 from S.E. China. Produce 200 lbs. of nuts per tree at 5 years. Delicious eaten raw, dried or canned. Called Kwai mi. (See 7th from left on page 57.)

MULBERRY TREE
Kilika (silk)　クワ

Morus nigra L.

These are the long-lived trees from Asia that are used for food by the silk worms. The fruits are sweet and juicy. Another Mulberry—Wauke—was used to make tapa cloth.

SEA GRAPE　ココロバス

Coccolobis (Coccoloba) uvifera

Small evergreen tree found near the beach withstands salt spray. Has 8″ red veined leaves used as writing paper. The grapes turn purple and are made into jelly

UMBRELLA TREE　ブサヤ
Octopus Tree, Rubber Tree

Brassaia actinophylla,
syn. *Schefflera actinophylla*

From Australia this good looking tree has large red octopus like blooms radiating from the top, and shiny green handsome leaves that look like umbrellas.

MACADAMIA NUT, Queensland Nut　　マカダミア

Macadamia integrifolia

This native tree of Australia is a rapid grower, up to 50′ and often bears fruit after seven years.

E. W. Jordan planted the first Macadamia Nut tree in Hawaii in about 1890. It bore so well that eventually it produced an orchard of 2,000 trees on Oahu, 6,000 trees at Kona, Hawaii, others on Maui and Kauai. Now they are used for reforesting as well as grown commercially (95% on Big Island) for their nuts. These very hard round nuts which ripen throughout the year are delicious. They contain 70% fat and are a good source of vitamins and minerals. The handsome dark green leaves are used for decoration, dried or sprayed for the holidays, as some varieties have fine toothed edges like holly leaves. A big tree can be seen in the Park at King and Keeaumoku.

MAHOGANY モハガニ

Swietenia mahagoni (L.) Jacq.

An evergreen with dark red wood valued
for furniture, finishing houses, musical instruments, ships and cabinets.
Native of Florida Keys and the West Indies. Shade and street planting 40′ to 75′
tree with thick brownish scaled bark and
trunk, shiny dark green leaves 4″ to 8″,
woody ovoid 2″ to 4″ fruit which stand erect
on curved stem on branch. Picture taken
looking down Kalakaua at King Street,
small one also in Park at King and Keeaumoku, University of Hawaii.

MAMMEE APPLE

マミア

Mammea americana L.

This native of Tropical America and the West Indies has grown in Hawaiian yards for many years. Similar to the Kamani, its relative, it is a large handsome 60′ tree with 4″ to 8″ shiny leather-like leaves, white 1″ fragrant flowers, and spherical 3″ to 8″ fruits that have thick bark-like brown skin (note apples on tree above).

The pulp is orange colored, sweet tasting, and can be eaten raw or cooked. The flowers are used in Tropical America to flavor a liqueur called "Eau-de-Creole." In Mexico, the juice and seeds are used as insecticides. Large tree in Park at King and Keeaumoku Streets.

MANGO TREE, Manako

Mangifera indica L.

マンゴ

The first tree on Hawaii was planted by Don Marin. The Mango trees grow to be very large trees and their dense foliage furnish abundant shade. (Note Water Buffalo in center picture.) Originating in India, the Mango is known as the "king of fruits." In January tiny pinkish white or yellow flowers covered with hairs form on the branch tips. The fruits ripen sometime between March and October. The orange pulp is sweet tasting, juicy and in great demand for eating raw (even green ones), stewed, frozen, and in chutney. (Haden and Pirie are choice varieties.)

Some people are highly allergic to blooms and skin of Mango. It is a resinous tree with the gum and bark used medicinally. The young leaves on the tree are red or pale green. Leaves smell like turpentine when crushed. In Mexico they are used to clean teeth and harden the gums. Seen growing wild on windward side of the Pali.

MONKEYPOD TREE, Rain Tree, 'Ohai   アメリカネム

Samanea saman (Jacq.) Merr.

If you see huge canopied umbrella-like trees as you drive up to the Pali, go through a park, or seek some shade, you are probably viewing a Monkeypod tree.

This is the tree from which are carved those lovely leaf and calabash bowls. See lower left picture. The tiny pink puffs seen in the picture below usually bloom in the spring and summer. The fern-like leaves that close in the late afternoon and on cloudy days, drop in February and March when the long black pods are noticeable.

MOUNTAIN APPLE, Malay Apple, 'Ohi'a 'ai ヤマリンゴ

Eugenia malaccensis L.

It is said that the Mountain Apple had worked its way across the Pacific and into Hawaii before the discovery of North and South America. It was reportedly the only fruit growing here at the coming of the white man.

English investors commissioned Captain Bligh to procure edible plants from the Pacific Isles in 1793 for Jamaica. The Malay or Mountain Apple was one of these. According to Polynesian legend, the tree was sacred and temple idols were carved from its wood.

It is a native of Malaya. A lovely 50′ evergreen tree with handsome large green shiny leaves, and tiny cerise colored blossoms that look like wee shaving brushes. These pop out all over the trunk and limbs of the tree in the early spring. Soon the small apple develops. Its pulp is similar to the apple for which it is named. Grows in shady valleys and mountains—Sacred Falls, Waimano Gulch, Foster Gardens, State Hospital, Tantalus.

NORFOLK ISLAND PINE ノーフクマツ

Araucaria excelsa (Lamb.) R. Br.

This is a perfectly symmetrical evergreen tree that Captain Cook discovered. He found it on Norfolk Island, which is a small island between Fiji and Australia.

It so closely resembles the Cook Pine (see next page), that in young trees it is hard to distinguish them apart. The Norfolk Pine develops into a wider cone shape, and has more numerous and narrower leaf scales ½" long.

These are often used as Christmas trees both in Hawaii and on the Mainland where they are grown in pots.

There are also related Hoop Pines and Bunya Bunya trees. All can be seen in Foster Gardens. Norfolk Island Pines can be seen in many yards, University of Hawaii, State Hospital.

COOK PINE クック マツ

Araucaria columnaris (Forst.)
Hook, syn. *A. cookii* R. Br.

The Cook Pine is one of the 12 best reforesting trees in Hawaii. It comes from New Caledonia (Isle of Pines) and is called a Cook Pine because Captain Cook discovered it there. He said upon approaching the island: "They had the appearance of tall pines which occasioned my giving that name to the island."

Actually the trees do not have needles like a pine, but have overlapping scale-like leaves about ¼″ long. These tall trees—up to 200′ are used for masts on ships. They are often mistaken for their relative the Norfolk Island Pine. Seen on mountains, in forests, yards, Foster Gardens, University of Hawaii.

'OHI'A LEHUA　レフア

Metrosideros collina (Forst.)
Gray subsp.
polymorpha (Gaud.) Rock

First tree to appear on a new lava flow is a favorite native tree of Hawaii growing at 1,000 ft. to 9,000 ft. elevations. Some forms are small trees as those pictured above on Mauna Loa (note snow covered Mauna Kea in the background), but many are 100′ tall trees.

The Hawaiians believe that the groves of trees are sacred to Pele, the Goddess of Volcanoes. When angry, Pele destroys these groves with streams of lava. They say if a Lehua is picked on the way to the mountain, it will rain.

The trees have many flowers of bright red stamens ½″ to 1″ at branch ends. These are the flower of the island of Hawaii. They contain honey which is food for the 'Iiwi bird, a small scarlet bird matching the flowers. The Lehua is made into lovely leis.

The tree has hard, dark red wood used for paving blocks, ties, flooring and interior furnishings, furniture, and fuel.

OPIUMA, Manila Tamarind, Madras Thorn   キンキジュ

Pithecellobium dulce (Roxb.) Benth.
(*Pithecolobium*)

The Tropical American tree above is a White Opiuma (*f. albo variegatum*). It is used in yard plantings and landscaping, but the green variety is often found growing wild due to birds carrying the seeds. It is a low, thorny branched, wide spreading tree that resembles a Kiawe.

The variegated variety has green and white leaves, the white becoming more predominant part of the time which makes it interesting as an ornamental. Small white flowers and red twisted pods appear in the spring. The pods contain a white sweet-tasting pulp which encloses black seeds—used for leis. The pulp is used for fodder and a drink similar to lemonade. The seeds resemble opium explaining the Hawaiian name Opiuma. The wood is used for lumber. Dye and gum are made from the bark. All parts of the tree used medicinally. A lovely tree can be seen in front of the Kailua 1st National Bank, University of Hawaii.

PALM TREES
Coconut Tree, Coco Palm, Niu

ココヤシ

Cocos nucifera L.

There are many species of palms, so only a few are noted. The Coco Palm is the best known, and one of the most beautiful palms in the world, its origin dating back to prehistoric times. They retain their germinating power 4 months after floating in the ocean. Growing to 100′, bearing over 40 fruits yearly at 6 years, they furnish food, oil for soaps, cosmetics, margarine, vitamin B; decorations, mats, hats, shelters, yards, midribs used for stalks for hibiscus, Kukui nuts.

ROYAL PALM ヤシ

Roystonea regia

A very stately native of Cuba named for Gen. Roy Stone, an American engineer in Puerto Rico. First in Hawaii was a seed Dr. G. P. Judd brought from West Indies in 1850. The trees are smooth ringed, light grey, with straight, majestic 60′ trunks, usually planted in rows. Mormon Temple, Elks Club.

QUEEN PALM, Feathery Coconut Palm, Monkey Nut ヤシ

Arecastrum romanzoffianum, syn. *Cocos plumosa*

Feathery plumes bedeck this 30′ to 60′ ornamental from South America. The 3′ to 6′ flowering clusters produce fruit with sweet tasting orange pulp. These are the "Monkey Nuts" that are used for leis and earrings. They have the same little monkey face the coconuts have (see 3rd from left on bracelet, page 57).

DATE PALM ナツメヤシ

Phoenix dactylifera L.

Prehistoric, date crop one of the oldest known—5,000 years. 800 uses—hats, mats, thatch, food, wine sugar. Probably from North Africa or India. Bears at 5 years until 200 years old. Requires little water. Bears 10,000 flowers in each cluster. 300 lbs. of dates to a tree. High in food value—50% sugar, 7% protein. Some Africans live on dates most of the year. Mohammed said to the Arabs: "Honor the date palm for it is your mother." Christendom's symbol of martyrdom or victory.

BLUE LATAN PALM

Latania loddigesii Mart.

ヤシ

This interesting fan palm from Africa and Mascarene Islands (Mauritius), is a fairly common ornamental in Hawaii. Its blue-green leaves 3' to 5' radiate from stems at the top of a trunk marked with rings. Only reaches a height of 20' here. Male and female flowers borne on separate trees. The female tree here has dark green ovoid fruits about 3" long. These are used for jewelry (see 6th from left, page 57).

PAPAYA, Pawpaw, Mikana, He'i   パパイヤ

Carica papaya L.

There are 45 species of Papaya. One of the favorite fruits in Hawaii. The trees are small, up to 25', and are one of the fastest growing trees. They will bear fruit when one year old. Some varieties weigh up to 8 lbs., but the Solo Papaya, a favorite in Hawaii, only weighs about 1½ lbs.—see picture at left. The Papaya groves can be seen when driving around the islands. The trees have 2' branches with 2' deeply lobed leaves clustered at the top of a hollow tapering trunk. Directly at the base of this umbrella-like cluster are the fruits which develop from creamy white 5-petaled fragrant flowers. Some trees produce fruit bearing flowers, some only pollen bearing (flowers used for leis), some produce both.

There are many uses for the orange sweet juicy pulp—drinks, jelly, food. It is a good source of vitamins A, C and G. Juice contains papain, a protein digestive tapped from green fruits and dried—Ceylon and West Indies supply most of this. Leaves used as soap, meat tenderizer. Seeds used medicinally.

PAPER BARK
Cajeput Tree カユプテ

Melaleuca leucadendron L.

Trees in background above are natives of S.E. Asia to Australia. Used for reforesting and landscaping. Unusual because of many layers of peeling spongy bark, narrow alternate leaves 2″ to 8″ long with branches continuing to grow beyond the flower spike and bearing new sets of leaves. Flowers grow on spikes 2″ to 6″ long, and as they die they leave fruits that form tiny dried rosettes.

KOA HAOLE ギンゴウカン

Leucaena glauca

The small trees in the foreground above are a common roadside weed of the Mimosa family. They have many uses. Pods and leaves make high protein fodder; the seeds of the brown pods seen near the center above are made into jewelry, belts, purses and mats. These are often combined with grey Job's Tears, Wili-Wili, etc.

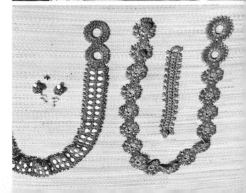

ROSE APPLE, Jambu, ‘Ohi‘a loke

フトモモ

Eugenia jambos L.

Native of India and Malaya thought to be the tree representing the theory of creation that bore the golden fruit of immortality. Buddha is sometimes pictured under the tree.

The 30′ evergreen tree, relative of the Mountain Apple (see page 45), has narrow pointed leaves, large greenish white pompon flowers that grow at the end of the branches in the spring, egg sized rose apple fruits with the sepals still clinging to them (see above). The fruit has a rose-water taste and odor which persists even in jelly. Mauka side of 1000 block on Kinau Street, also on Molokai.

ROYAL POINCIANA, Flame Tree, Flamboyant, 'Ohai, 'Ula

ローヤルポンシナ

Delonix regia (Bojer) Raf.

The Poinciana is one of the most strikingly beautiful trees of the world. Like a huge scarlet umbrella, it bursts into dense clusters of blossoms early in spring that last until late summer. Each bloom has five petals, one of which is white or yellow. It has fern-like leaves and long brown pods that hang on the tree long after the flowers have disappeared. The seeds from these pods are strung into leis. The tree is a member of the Legume family from Madagascar. Wilder Avenue, Lusitana, Kalihi at Dillingham Avenue.

SANDALWOOD, 'Iliahi

サンタラム

Santalum

The Chinese formerly called Hawaii the "Sandalwood Islands" because from about 1790 to 1840 there were many natural groves of Sandalwood that were exported. The Chinese used it for temple incense, furniture, etc. It was one of the first profitable export trades in Hawaii. Today, few trees can be found on Oahu. There is a small one in Foster Gardens. The government is trying to increase plantings. In 1932 they planted 1,000 *S. album* seedlings. Trees are scattered in some forests in Hawaii. The tree is partly parasitic, and is usually set out near host trees of Koa or Ironwood. Sandalwood is one of the most costly of woods. It is used for chests, furniture, medicine, perfume, oil, food.

SAND-BOX TREE, ヒウラ
Hura

Hura crepitans L.

A large deciduous spiny tree from the West Indies, Central and South America, with poisonous milky sap which could cause blindness. It has ovate, heart-shaped leaves, a dark maroon flower, and fruits like tiny 3″ pumpkins (see close-up above— also right below). Each contain 15 to 20 divisions with round flat seeds that explode when ripe. These are the curious parts of the tree.

In Hawaii, the split seeds are used for leis and jewelry (see right end of bracelet below). Also the entire fruit (right) was used as a container for sand for blotting letters and paper weights. University of Hawaii.

SAUSAGE TREE　キギリア

Kigelia pinnata (Jacq.) DC.
Syn. *K. africana* (Lam.) Benth.

This good sized, wide spreading tree 30′ high or more is a native of Tropical West Africa. Grown mainly for its curious, odd, large sausage-shaped fruits 12″ to 20″ by 3″ to 6″ that dangle from the branches for many months.

Large wine colored flowers that bloom at night and have a rather unpleasant odor hang down on cord-like strings and drop each morning after flowering (see close-up above). Then the funny grey sausages develop. They are not edible but are used externally for medicine in Africa. Seen in Foster Gardens, University of Hawaii, N. Kalaheo in Kailua, Leeward near Makaha, and at Trader Hall's on Windward Side.

SILK OAK, Silky Oak, Silver Oak, He Oak, Oka Kilika, Ha'iku, Ke'oke'o シノブノキ

Grevillea robusta A. Cunn.

Another one of the 12 best reforesting trees in Hawaii is this tall, interesting tree from Australia called the Silky Oak. The leaves are fern-like with long dark leaflets, like a small palm. It has unusual dark yellow feathery blooms that jut out all over the tree from early spring until fall.

It is a fast growing tree up to 100' tall. The wood is similar to oak thus giving it the name Silk Oak. The seeds germinate easily so the tree can be seen dotted here and there in our Hawaiian forests. Many behind Schofield, Ewa of Pali Freeway, University of Hawaii, all islands.

SKUNK TREE ステクリア
Java Olives, Kelumpang

Sterculia foetida L.

A deciduous tree from the Old World that has red, yellow or purple flowers which give the tree a pinkish-coral color when in full bloom. These flowers have a very unpleasant odor hence the name "Skunk Tree." The leaves 5″ to 11″ are cut into the stem. They are used medicinally. The handsome fruits (see close up) are most useful for dried or spray painted arrangements. They have 1 to 5 scarlet 3″ sections resembling cupped hands. As the ripe capsules gap open, they reveal 10 to 15 smooth black 1″ olive-like seeds that are edible but have a purgative effect. Univ. of Hawaii, Kaneohe Bay Drive (Makai), near end of Kailua Road. Similar tree—Gular (*S. urens*) in Thomas Square.

SOURSOP, Katu-anoda

Annona (Anona) muricata L.

A small evergreen W. Indies tree with fragrant laurel-like leaves and unusual kidney shaped prickly fruits weighing up to 6 lbs. A sweet-sour juice is extracted from the fruit's white pulp which makes pleasant cooling drinks and ices. Fruits are eaten by stock. Haiku Gardens, University of Hawaii.

SURINAM CHERRY, French Cherry, Pitanga　タチバナアデク

Eugenia uniflora Linnaeus

A nicely shaped small tree from Brazil, often grown as an ornamental. It has small shiny oval leaves with inconspicuous small white fragrant flowers. The fruit is bright red, waxy looking, with 8 little furrows forming small ovate spicy edible 1″ cherries that make good jelly. University of Hawaii.

TECOMA TREE　タベブイア
Pink Tecoma, Amapa,
Roble Blanco, White Cedar

Tabebuia pentaphylla (L.) Hemsl.

The Pink Tecoma from Tropical America is a cousin to the larger Gold Tree (see page 24). It is used extensively for yard and curbside plantings. Of the Bignonia family, the 20′ to 60′ tree resembles a bouquet of pinkish, lavender petunia-like trumpets. It will flower before it is two. The light gray-brown wood is used for house finishings. It resembles oak—Roble means oak. Many trees in Dowsett Highlands, along Kainalu Drive in Kailua.

TIGER'S CLAW, Indian Coral Tree, Wili-Wili Haole ヘリトリナ

Erythrina indica Lamarck, syn. *E. variegata* var. *orientalis* (L.) Merr.

This rather large spreading deciduous tree from India and Asia bursts with scarlet flowers in January and February. As the leaves fall, these claw shaped blooms are borne in tufts at the tips of the branches. The seed pods, too, resemble feline claws. They house a dark red seed used for leis in Hawaii similar to the bright red seeds of the tree called Wili-Wili by the natives (*E. monosperma* or *E. sanwicensis*). Erythrina is from the Greek word meaning red. However, the smaller bright round seeds so commonly seen in jewelry in Hawaii come from the False Wili-Wili. (See page 23.) Trees can be seen left on entering Kailua, slopes of Tantalus, Iolani Palace, University of Hawaii grounds, on way to Oahu Country Club, Castle High School.

Additional flowering trees, as well as the flowers of Hawaii, are pictured in full color in a companion book, "Hawaii Blossoms"—*Hargreaves*. This volume contains over 100 full color pictures of the flowers and flowering trees of Hawaii with authentic descriptions. 64 pages. It can be obtained at retail counters everywhere in Hawaii.

TRAVELLER'S TREE, Traveller's Palm

Ravenala madagascariensis J. F. Gme

A thirsty traveller can always find a drin in a Traveller's Tree. The leaves on th trunk have long thick overlapping stem which store a quart or more of wate Although the tree resembles a palm, belongs to the Banana Family. Its flower leaves, and fruits are similar to its cousi the White Bird of Paradise. The popula orange "Birds" and Heliconia also belon to this family. These can all be foun pictured in "Hawaii Blossoms," *Hargreave* The tree is a native of Madagascar. Ca be seen at Foster Gardens, University Hawaii, on Kapiolani Blvd. above Piik Street.

Publications by the same authors:

All books in this family are 64 pages each, all have over 100 full color pictures (some as many as 130) and all are the same size and format. Local names in local languages and text are different to reflect the countries and geographical areas they cover. Botanical names are included.

- "TROPICAL BLOSSOMS of the CARIBBEAN"
- "TROPICAL TREES found in the CARIBBEAN, South America, Central America, Mexico"
- "AFRICAN BLOSSOMS" (covers Tropical Africa, South Africa, Madagascar, Mauritius)
- "AFRICAN TREES" (covers same areas as "African Blossoms")

- "HAWAII BLOSSOMS"
- "TROPICAL TREES of HAWAII"
- "TROPICAL BLOSSOMS of the PACIFIC" (covers S.E. Asia, Malaysia, Ceylon and Pacific Ocean countries)
- "TROPICAL TREES of the PACIFIC" (covers same areas as "Tropical Blossoms of the Pacific")

All books can generally be found in book stores and tourist shops in the particular countries they cover. Or, books will be mailed postage paid via surface mail anywhere in the world for $5.50 each in U.S. funds from the publisher:

ROSS-HARGREAVES

P.O. Box 11897 Lahaina, Hawaii 96761 U.S.A.
IMPORTANT: If AIR MAIL delivery *outside* the U.S.A. or territories is desired, add $3.90 U.S. for one copy, plus $2.50 for each additional copy to cover extra airmail postage. If AIR MAIL delivery *inside* the U.S. or territories is desired, add $3.00 for up to six copies, plus $2.00 for each additional two copies.
When ordering from outside the U.S.A. please send payment with order in U.S. currency, International Postal Money Order, Bank Draft, or check on any U.S. bank.

Lithographed in Japan